W9-CFD-795

Congratulations!
Now that you'll be Ed.
for the first grandchild
maybe we can go all of us
Down East —
Love Linda   April 25, 1990

EXPLORING THE
MAINE COAST

SUNRISE, SEAL BAY, VINALHAVEN ISLAND

MOONRISE, BIRCH POINT, SOUTH THOMASTON

EXPLORING THE
MAINE COAST

PHOTOGRAPHS AND TEXT BY
ALAN NYIRI

DOWN EAST BOOKS
CAMDEN, MAINE

OTHER DOWN EAST BOOKS BY ALAN NYIRI:

Acadia National Park: Maine's Intimate Parkland

The White Mountains of New Hampshire

Copyright © 1989 by Alan Nyiri
ISBN 0-89272-256-8

Design and Layout by Alan Nyiri
Composition: Typeworks, Belfast, Maine
Printing and binding: Palace Press, San Francisco, Calif.
Printed in Singapore

2   4   5   3   1

Down East Books
Camden, Maine

To
My editor, Leon H. Ballou,
with gratitude and affection.
His encouragement and assistance
made it possible for me to
embark on three great adventures,
published as books by his firm.

PREFACE

I was about eleven years old when I discovered the Maine coast. My family had been vacationing in Maine for years, but since my parents were "lake people," we rented a small cottage in the Tacoma Lake region each August. My mom relaxed by the lake shore, my older sister explored the intricacies of summer society, and my dad and I fished for smallmouth bass. As far as my family was concerned, this lake was our personal Shangri-la, and we never ventured far from it.

Then one cool, drizzly Saturday, my parents decided to take the family on a day trip down to Orrs and Bailey islands, our first trip to the Maine coast. Although the weather forecast had called for clearing, the sky was still dismally overcast as we crossed the Cobwork Bridge onto Bailey Island. Mom was disappointed when we arrived. The fog that engulfed the coast, reducing visibility to almost nothing, was exactly the reason she had hesitated to come to the shore in years past. But the tide was out, and my dad and I wanted to explore the tide pools, so we stayed to picnic.

While the blanket of fog distressed my mother, it provided a source of mystery and intrigue for my fertile pre-adolescent mind. As we searched the tidepools for sea urchins, starfish, and rock crabs hiding in the rockweed, I half expected a ghostly pirate ship to emerge from the fog. Everything here was new to me in experience, but familiar from books I'd read. Here were the acorn barnacles I had watched on television, feeding with their feathery comb-shaped arms until low tide forced them to lock their shells closed. Here also were the other fascinating creatures I had long wanted to observe directly: sea anemones, which looked like short, stocky flowers but were actually animals that ate by stinging their prey with their petallike tentacles; a starfish, which used the suckers on its arms to slowly pull apart the shells of a mussel and then everted its stomach through its mouth to digest its prey; and the rockweeds, which had evolved gas-filled bladders to buoy up the plant during high water to expose its fronds to sunlight.

Sometime after lunch, a slight breeze stirred from the west and the fog started to lift almost imperceptibly. From behind a thick veil of swirling fog the sun cast a strange opalescent light over our shore. The fresh breeze carried the tangy scent of the ocean: the smell of salt and life and death. As the fog thinned and lifted, shapes began to emerge and take form, fascinating because I had no idea of what to expect. A murky shadow slowly took form as a treeless, rocky island. Another shadow appeared, gliding through the mists accompanied by a steady "lub – lub – lub" sound; a lobsterman, taking advantage of the clearing weather, was out in his boat checking his traps. Overhead, herring gulls swooped and squawked, looking for an easy meal. I remember the excitement I felt as the mist-shrouded world gradually expanded, first revealing the immediate stony shore, then the nearby islands, and finally the vast sweep of coastline and the infinite sea beyond. Simply put, I was in my boyhood Heaven that day.

I could not know it at the time, of course, but that day began perhaps the longest love affair I'll ever know, my *affaire de coeur* with the coast of Maine. I would not return until my college years, when a summer job tending buoys in the Maine lakes nonetheless found me spending weekends on the southern beaches instead of fishing for bass in the lakes. After college, I spent several years traveling around the country trying to come to grips with my newfound profession, photography, but I eventually returned to the Maine coast looking for work. A fruitless search led me back to the lakes again, this time as a modern-day lumberjack on Moosehead Lake for a winter.

During the next ten years I would visit the Maine coast only infrequently, for I was preoccupied with establishing myself as a photographer and businessman. However, in 1983 I was able to return and combine my passions for Maine and photography. I enrolled in a workshop at the Maine Photographic Workshop in Rockport, and that excellent program quickly rekindled both passions. Returning the following summer to participate in a workshop with photographer Eliot Porter, I discovered a means to unite both loves: a self-imposed assignment to photograph the Maine coast. For the next four years I would return to the coast as often as my work schedule would permit, making at least a dozen trips to all sections of the coastline. Several of these trips centered on Acadia National Park, for Down East Books had commissioned me to produce a book about this wonderful park. The success of that book led directly to the labor of love you now hold in your hands.

After logging several thousand miles of driving along this beautiful coastline in all seasons, I can still scarcely claim to know it well. Although I have traveled from Kittery to Lubec and back several times – a distance of about three hundred miles – I have really only begun to explore the intricacies of this coast. For every place I have visited, at least ten more remain to be explored. If you were to follow the shoreline in a boat, meandering along all the bays, peninsulas, and estuaries, your trip would measure almost three thousand miles when completed. And while hundreds of little side roads fan out from the main roads, much of the coast, with its countless fascinating niches, is still inaccessible by car.

Even though I've tried to visit as much of the Maine coast as I could, certain areas seem to call me back again and again. Perhaps they hold the promise of unlocking the quintessential secret of Maine's allure; perhaps as I continue to explore the coves and marshes, islands and peninsulas, I will at last discover that secret and capture it on film.

EXPLORING THE MAINE COAST

SOUTHERN SHORES

PASSING SHOWER, OLD ORCHARD BEACH

EARLY MORNING, LONG BEACH, YORK

MORNING STROLLERS, LONG BEACH, YORK

SUNRISE, SCARBOROUGH MARSH

DAWN, SCARBOROUGH MARSH

NUBBLE LIGHT, CAPE NEDDICK, YORK

LOW TIDE, OLD ORCHARD BEACH

LOBSTER BOATS, SCARBOROUGH RIVER, PINE POINT

MARSH GRASSES, SEAPOINT, KITTERY POINT

JUICE STAND, OLD ORCHARD OCEAN PIER

BUILDING STORM, OLD ORCHARD BEACH

ROCKS BORDERING HILLS BEACH, BIDDEFORD POOL

SHIPWRECK REMAINS, HIGGENS BEACH, SCARBOROUGH

SEAPOINT MARSH, KITTERY POINT

EVENING AT MASSACRE POND, SCARBOROUGH BEACH

SOFT LIGHT

BEACH PEA AND COBBLES, MARTINSVILLE

SUNSET OVER DUCK HARBOR, ISLE AU HAUT

ROADSIDE FOLIAGE NEAR DENNYSVILLE

FISHING BOATS OFF PEMAQUID POINT

HEN ISLAND, SEAL BAY, VINALHAVEN ISLAND

31

COBBLES AND BEDROCK SCHIST, PEMAQUID POINT

SEAWALL AT LUCIA BEACH, SOUTH THOMASTON

FIREWEED AT ALLEY POINT, GREAT WASS ISLAND

MOONRISE, OTTER POINT, ACADIA NATIONAL PARK

MORNING LIGHT ON YELLOW BARN, CUTLER

DAYLILIES, SOUTHWEST HARBOR

DRIFTING SNOW ON JORDAN POND, ACADIA NATIONAL PARK

FRACTURES IN BASALTIC DIKE, SCHOODIC PENINSULA

DETAIL IN THE BEDROCK SCHIST, PEMAQUID POINT

RUGOSA ROSE AND VETCH, PEMAQUID POINT

BAYS, NECKS, AND COVES: THE MIDCOAST

STONINGTON HARBOR IN FOG

SUNSET, PEMAQUID BEACH

FINNISH CONGREGATIONAL CHURCH, ST. GEORGE

RACKLIFF ISLAND AND BAY, SPRUCE HEAD

LUCIA BEACH, SOUTH THOMASTON

STINSON NECK, DEER ISLE

COBBLES AND BEDROCK SCHIST, LOW TIDE, PEMAQUID POINT

LOBSTER POTS, NEW HARBOR

LOBSTERMAN'S SHED, STONINGTON

SUNSET OVER PULPIT ROCK, NORTH HAVEN ISLAND

CLEARING STORM, PEMAQUID POINT

LIGHTHOUSE AT DAWN, PEMAQUID POINT

ABANDONED FISHING BOAT AND DAY-SAILERS, PORT CLYDE

SEA SMOKE AND SEGUIN ISLAND LIGHT, POPHAM BEACH

FIRST LIGHT ON BIRCH POINT, SOUTH THOMASTON

LOW TIDE

CEDAR STUMP, MOSQUITO HEAD, MARTINSVILLE

LOW TIDE ALONG WHITING BAY, COBSCOOK BAY STATE PARK

GRAVEL BAR ON SCHOODIC PENINSULA, ACADIA NATIONAL PARK

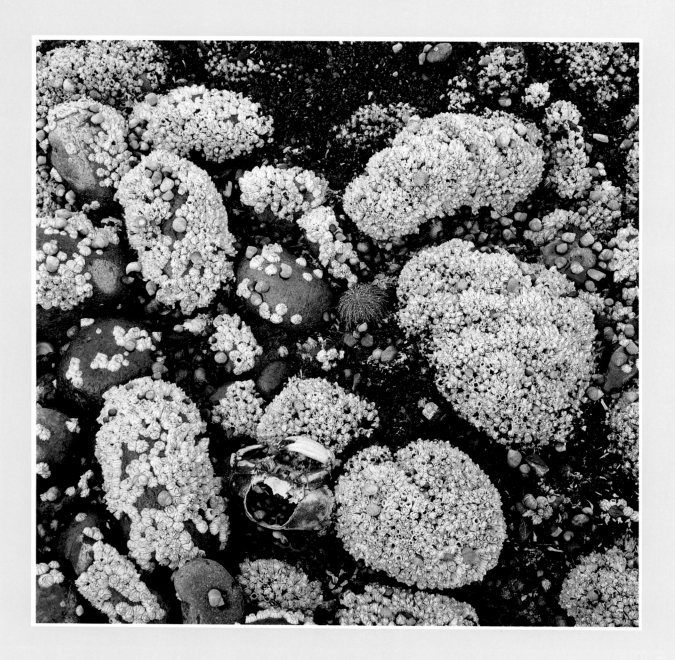

BARNACLES AND CRAB SHELL, ISLE AU HAUT

MUSSEL FLAT AND TIDAL POOL, ISLE AU HAUT

64   ROCKWEED AT PENDLETON POINT, ISLESBORO ISLAND

GLACIAL ERRATIC, BURNT COVE, COBSCOOK BAY STATE PARK

GROUNDED SARDINER *FISH HAWK*, GREAT WASS ISLAND

RUDDER DETAIL, *FISH HAWK*, GREAT WASS ISLAND

ROCK "GARDEN" AT LUCIA BEACH, SOUTH THOMASTON

FOG BURNING OFF, LONG BEACH, YORK

MUD RIPPLES, LONG BEACH, YORK

HIGH-WATER MARK, THOMPSON ISLAND, ACADIA NATIONAL PARK

REFLECTIONS, OLD ORCHARD BEACH

HEN ISLAND, SEAL BAY, VINALHAVEN ISLAND

THE ACADIAN COASTLINE

SUNRISE FROM ANEMONE CAVE, ACADIA NATIONAL PARK

NEWPORT COVE FROM OTTER CLIFFS, ACADIA NATIONAL PARK

FERNS AND SPRUCE BLOWDOWNS, ISLE AU HAUT

OTTER POINT FROM CADILLAC MOUNTAIN, ACADIA NATIONAL PARK

PICKEREL WEED ON EAGLE LAKE, ACADIA NATIONAL PARK

FRACTURED GRANITE, SCHOODIC PENINSULA, ACADIA NATIONAL PARK

MONUMENT COVE IN FOG, ACADIA NATIONAL PARK

LUPINE NEAR SALISBURY COVE, MT. DESERT ISLAND

DAWN AT OTTER CLIFFS, ACADIA NATIONAL PARK

WINTER SURF NEAR SHIP HARBOR, ACADIA NATIONAL PARK

MOONRISE OVER OTTER CLIFFS, ACADIA NATIONAL PARK

GRANITE COBBLES, HUNTER'S COVE, ACADIA NATIONAL PARK

BALD PORCUPINE ISLAND IN FOG FROM BAR HARBOR

JORDAN POND AND THE BUBBLES, ACADIA NATIONAL PARK

AUTUMN LIGHT, CHAMPLAIN MOUNTAIN, ACADIA NATIONAL PARK

SNOW ON COBBLE BOULDERS, OTTER POINT, ACADIA NATIONAL PARK

JANUARY DAWN, OTTER CLIFFS, ACADIA NATIONAL PARK

TRANSITIONS

RAINDROPS ON COBBLES, OTTER POINT, ACADIA NATIONAL PARK

LAST RUGOSA ROSE BLOSSOM OF THE SEASON, PEMAQUID BEACH

INTERRUPTED FERNS, BLACKWOODS, ACADIA NATIONAL PARK

DRIFTING SAND AND SNOW CRYSTALS, POPHAM BEACH

FIRST LIGHT ON THE BEEHIVE, ACADIA NATIONAL PARK

BALD HEAD CLIFFS AT LOW TIDE, OGUNQUIT

AUTUMN TOUCHES A BLACKWATER POND NEAR SOUTH BRISTOL

FOG INVADES BASS HARBOR, FROM THE WHARF IN BERNARD

WINDOW OF THE J.H. BUTTERFIELD CO. MARKET, BAR HARBOR

DEAD SPRUCE, PULPIT HARBOR, NORTH HAVEN ISLAND

DYING BALSAM FIR, ROCKPORT

104   ROADSIDE GARDEN OF WILDFLOWERS, ROCKPORT

ABANDONED FARMHOUSE ON HERSEY NECK, PEMBROKE

WAY DOWN EAST

LIFTING FOG, SAWYER COVE, JONESPORT

FIELD BY HAMILTON COVE, NEAR WEST QUODDY HEAD

GULLIVER'S HOLE, WEST QUODDY HEAD

CUMULUS CLOUDS, BAR ISLAND, JONESPORT

WHITING BAY, COBSCOOK BAY STATE PARK

BLUEBERRY BARRENS IN AUTUMN, COLUMBIA FALLS

CANNING FACTORIES ON WHARF, STONINGTON

WHARF IN FOG, BEAL ISLAND

LOBSTER BOAT IN HAMILTON COVE, GRAND MANAN IN DISTANCE

LOBSTER BOATS, CUTLER HARBOR

RUSTING STEEL DRUMS, CUTLER

LUBEC CHANNEL LIGHT AND CANNERY, LUBEC

MASONIC TEMPLE, CUTLER

LOBSTER TRAP BUOYS, BEAL ISLAND

AGING BUILDING AT FIFIELD POINT, STONINGTON

About the Photographs

The photographic images in this book were made with a Sinar-F view camera and a variety of Schneider and Nikkor lenses with focal lengths from 70mm to 500mm. I find that a large format camera mounted on a sturdy tripod is essential for this kind of landscape photography: images are not only easier to reproduce crisply from a large 4-by-5-inch transparency, but are also easier to previsualize and compose on the large ground glass of the camera. Kodak's Ektachrome 64 and 100 daylight transparency films were used throughout this project. I made exposure calculations with the help of a Minolta 1-degree spot meter, exposing to retain highlight detail in most cases.

EVENING, STONINGTON HARBOR